Chambers of an Open Heart

Tenesha Hawkins

Acknowledgments

Thank you to my Mom who believed in me and my writing even when I didn't believe in myself. Thank you for teaching me how to be a woman of excellence and to love sincerely, with everything I am. Most importantly, I want to thank God for the book of The Songs of Solomon in the Bible, which is where I've drawn most of my inspiration to write this book.

Contents

Praying Man 1
Questions to the Bridegroom 3
Presence 5
Vats of my Soul 7
I Would 9
Something so Real 10
Wildfire 13
I Search for You 15
Caramel Macchiato Coffee 16
African Blackwood (Ode to Black Men) 20
An Ocean of Things 23
You 27
Songs of You 29
Geometry 30
Morning Dinner 32
Let 33
Tsunami Skin 34
Wonder and Grenades 35
Make Love Like 39
Until the Thunder Rolls 41

Praying Man

You are a praying man
You have an orchard in your throat
Daily offering God the fruit of your lips
You intercede
Bombarding heaven with what you believe until demons bleed
You have managed to fit an entire kingdom on the width of your tongue
You alter an atmosphere with the shift of your lungs
You turn a conversation into an Autobahn

Beckoning angels to your bedside
Until they overflow on your front lawn
You speak words of another dimension
You cut off senses to get heaven's attention
You are a threat
One of the reasons that I am blessed
You are a warrior whose sword is never at rest
A tongue, a tone, a breath of biblical warfare arresting the angel of death

You are soft carpet and bended knees
A loaded chamber of faith allowing Holy Spirit to squeeze
With your mouth you eradicate every lie that the devil will fabricate

Your throat is a fire escape
You speak and then fire escapes
You carry a realm with God at the helm, so it's quite understandable
You are the handiwork of God— chiseled is the art of your mandible—
Strong enough to carry a prayer, shout praise,
Bless God, free slaves

And the heat of your kiss
Comes from standing face to face with hell
And then slicing its wrists
You are triumphant
A heavenly servant at his summit
With God on a cliff of confidence where pride will plummet
And we kneel side by side like two barrels of a shot gun
Ready for war
Yet thanking God for what's already done
And whatever's in store

You are more than thighs squeezing tight like a kid
Learning to ride his bike with no hands for the first time
You are a man that prays
And because the Lord was willing
You're mine.

Questions to the Bridegroom

To the Bridegroom
to the only man who loves me enough
to stretch his arms wide enough
to hug death on my behalf.
When you resurrected yourself,
Did your first breath taste like my laugh?
Were your bones not broken so that we could dance
like the shoulders of a lion?
Remember when we bathed in a sheet of the horizon—
when my face flashed before your eyes
as you gazed into your cup
and decided not to let it pass
Because I'd be lost without your love?

Does your goodness and mercy stretch before it chases me down?
With broken skin,
Did you forgive my sin before your blood could hit the ground?
Was your hardest decision to lay down your life
or to make me your wife—
to dress me in your image and place a ring around my heart,

So that I could now rejoice inside your love as if I never knew the dark?
How great is your love that it takes a lifetime and an eternity to receive
And your Spirit so committed that it vows to never leave?
How great is your love that it saves me from myself,
and, Jesus, your name
the most glorious thing my lungs have ever felt?

Presence

I want that feeling you give me,
that my breath matters because I get to use it to voice the fiery power of your name.
The woman I want to be is possible when you're in the room.
You are the better version of the best version of everything good,
I want you here because everything in me responds to you,
Every cell and atom is intoxicated with the perfection of your presence,
Every ounce of my being obeys the demand your beauty puts on the atmosphere of my anatomy
Loose-legged, dropped-jawed, I'm at a loss for words,
I want more of you,
All of you,
Where I am.
I've got to be in your presence.

To be near you shifts the pattern of my galaxy,
And I daydream about how I would split the sky open and squeeze the sun,
All over the horizon until the rays became daring enough
to drink the radiance,

Spilling from your complexion
Just to be next to you.
I'm just a tourist,
Walking on the tar paved streets of time
In the corridors of consciousness,
Contemplating your awesomeness—
You've made everything from a blade of grass,
To joyful, tear-filled eyes that look like glass,
And I am beckoning you to walk from now to eternity with me,
Where a day with you is like a thousand and a thousand is like a day.

Vats of my Soul

When the vats of my soul have run dry
And I don't have enough discipline to even cry,
When the cares of this life rush in
to blister the feet of my patience that's running thin,
When ecstasy's in the shape of a pen
And jealousy's in the shape of a friend,
When the world would rather lie but rather not be called a liar,
I reach within to hold your fire,

Because you are greater than high tides and mudslides,
Tornadoes, weary souls and hateful foes,
So lifted hands are just my soldier stance
I swing the sword and then my life's enhanced,
There's no greater love for which I'd rather die
But to die for you is gain, I find I hardly cry.
Anything you've ever done is grounds for worship,
Indeed the Word captures the heart of a wordsmith.

What do you give a gift?
How heavy is a holy name, yet still I dare to lift?
So whatever I am facing
is just a ghost compared to what it is that I am

tasting—
the honey of your song over my spirit.
Your lyrics and your tone cologne wherever your voice visits
So let my song to you be a single note
within the fragrance of your beauty,
And my heart will devote every chamber to always love you truly.
Yes, my heart will devote every chamber to always love you truly.

I Would

I'd place my head upon your chest
so that I could have your heartbeats teach me the
right way to love myself—
the way you love me.
I'd walk on water just to get to you and rescue you
from drowning in the jealousy of your enemies.
I'd wet my feet with the ocean of faith it takes for
every ounce of me to trust you.
I'd turn water into wine
just to drink from the same cup as you
and get drunk off of the moistness of your lips.
I'd pour the oil of your laughter all over my skin
like I was bathing in the brightness of your inner
splendor.
I'd pour oil.
I'd pour.
I'd pour liquid lilies between the valleys of your
toes
so that you would know there is a meadow with
me
where we both drink from the well of life.

Something so Real

It's one of those wet popsicle nights
Where we sit in the trunk of my truck and watch
the sky slip into something more comfortable
Until it is wearing nothing but the moon
And I gaze as the stars bury themselves in your teeth like graves
Because they grew tired of living in anything less than the heaven
Hovering between your lips.
To kiss you is like slicing open the sun
And finding God waiting with a warm hug in the inside.

You make my tongue wet with a thousand sunsets smashed into your smile,
There is everlasting and infinity inside the grin that you house
And I've never called a man beautiful before,
But you are beautiful
And I'm sure that God sprays two squirts of your reflection on His wrists
Before He pushes the ocean up to the seashore's lips,
And fills the living room of every sand castle with a stream
After burying the bass line of your voice in every dream.

So when you ask me what I want to do,
I want to hold you so close that I could write your autobiography,
And make love to you
Until our bodies shake like there are tambourines in our navels,
But we are merely friends
And my heart is full of "Let's take it there"
But your belly is full of I can'ts
And I can understand not wanting to jeopardize something so real,
So I guess I'll pretend to not feel what I feel.

I guess I'll pretend I don't want to skinny dip in the heat of your hands
Or to horseback ride in your memories
On the beach of your plans.
I guess I'll pretend I don't want you to lie in my hair
With the strength of my soul by your side,
To hold your hand as we undress your fears
In the face of your pride.
I'll pretend like I'm not being blinded
By the constellations that have been birthed in your gums,
Or that you don't make my spine sweat until it succumbs
To the thousands of sunrises embedded in the prints of your thumbs.

But I can understand not wanting to jeopardize something so real,
So I guess I'll pretend
Not to feel what I feel.

Wildfire

We could be a wildfire
But instead we sit here like matchsticks—
Never knowing what it's like to kindle something
worth burning for—
Harnessing all of this flame inside,
Sitting on the edge of extinguished and alive.

I run into the rivers of your aroma
Where my mind explodes with the desire of your
persona,
My eyes are always a slave to my hunger for your
smile,
Birthing beauty in the belly of my brain
So I labor with the thought of you for quite a while.

But, see, thoughts only hold like eyes do,
Where you're basking in the basket of an image
But hands turn spines goo,
Because a touch is all intents and fingerprints,
And a body is a tangible substance when enough's
said.

So scold me with your presence—
Darken my doorway and let your light stay.
You are a swan over a pond on a bright day.
My heart is loaded—

Fascinated by your caliber and how we could have exploded,

But everything happens for a reason,
And God always knows what's best—
So we are dust and when the dust settles you're still a trigger in my chest.

I Search for You

I searched for you on my college campus
and I pledged to the Alpha and Omega,
that if I found you I would treat you like release day
from my penitentiary of loneliness.
I looked for you on Sunday mornings,
hoping I could breathe in the sweet fragrance of
your prayers for me.
I checked for you at the mall,
but I didn't count the cost of how much shopping
I'd have to do
to find only pieces of you in other men who could
never fit.
I sought after you in my poems,
scuba dived into every stanza, flung open the door
of every metaphor,
trying to grasp your fingers and feel the gravity of
your bones over my bones.
Sometimes I wonder why love is so heavy,
but I shoulder my longing for you and keep
pressing upward.

Caramel Macchiato Coffee

To the guy sitting by the window at Starbucks,
logged into Facebook, slumping over his laptop like a street lamp
because he has 2,000 friends and no one to talk to,
I just want to tell you
I'm sitting at the table across from you, sipping a caramel macchiato,
writing you a love letter.

It reads,
"You are an angel
and I just want to strap your veins to a violin
to duplicate the sound of heaven beating in your chest.
You make me want to jump off of the tallest skyscraper
and land in the depth of your chest
so I can scream I love you from the balcony of my lungs
until I am covered in the avalanche of your heartbeats.
I just want to love you
and remind you that you are a king
and that your chair is a throne holding more than just a human being.

1 Your irises are stained glass windows hugging the light from the embers burning in your soul.
2 Your voice is a galaxy of gravity, thunder, and wild orchids.
3 Your face is the basement of a wishing well,
It is rich
And one dimension away from being an actual prayer.
4 Believe me.
5 Believe me,
Something as beautiful as you humbly comes before God
and freezes in the fist of an angel,
Spends the night between the knuckles of the moon
before unthawing in the emptiness of God's collarbone,
Leaving a pool of your depth
until He is wearing the cool of your breath.

You are a sunflower preaching to a meadow full of dandelions
on how to keep their faces to the sun,
Your soul is the ghost of a daffodil,
Bright like a tattoo painted between the shoulders of the sun,
Your breath is a Blue jay,
Your chest is a rose garden,
I wish my hands were a bouquet.

I've decided that I can't go another day
without blowing into the seashell of your
vertebrae.
Like a tropical breeze,
I just want to slow dance with you
on the seashore under a canopy until we both
smell like salt water,
And make love to you like a hurricane
moving in slow-motion.

If you were mine
I would remind you that you are loved by the
creator of comets,
And every fire in the sky,
And every deep desire that won't die.
So even if you're broken I will still remind you
that you have the breath of God
Walking, walking, walking
In the bottom of your lungs,
You have the breath of God walking in the bottom
of your lungs,
You are a king.
He breathed life into your nostrils and made you a
living being
So don't let those "friends" rob you of the peacock
pride you're entitled to.

I heard the best conversations start with hello.
From the attic of my lungs I love you,

I'd send my last breath to commit suicide on my tongue just to tell you
Hello.
Sincerely,
The girl across the way sipping the caramel macchiato."

African Blackwood (Ode to Black Men)

You are imported from heaven,
One of the truest of the true ebonies,
A musical instrument of glory,
Small pores upon your body whistle against the
lips of the sunlight constructing pearls under
the burn of the bright,
You—glossy jeweled strength,
You are a robe that a king would dawn at his
gate,
What I wouldn't give to be a doe lost among
the foliage of your forest.

The earth yawned and gave birth to you,
The sky opened its mouth and I found you,
like a wise woman whose camels are weighed
down
with the fine oils of her embraces,
the taste of her kisses, and the delicate dust
that she is.
Out of all the colors the night sky had to choose
from,
It chose to reflect your complexion to the
world,
Barking a question from a mystery—
the divine tapestry of your line's history—
"How beautiful is African Blackwood?"

When I speak, you grow,
When I breathe you know,
If I could fashion a bed with you,
or lie with your guitar,
What music we would make under the canopy
of creation,
What I wouldn't give to run my fingers along
the floors of your mansion,
and reveal in a whisper to my friends the
intense extent of your expense,
There are stories in your skin,

One day these rings within will be linked among
these twigs
that we grab life with,
Then the root of what our trunks rest upon
will be a jumbled jungle of sweat,
and a symphony of rhythm and song
Dance with me,
I want to be your whirlwind of desert heat—
the perfect climate for a lioness' nails and
teeth,
We are more than Evergreen when you stretch
your limbs over my everything,
What we do the winds have never seen
on this side of the heavenlies.

How brilliant?
How resilient
And everything in between,
or rather on the spectrum?
How much do I love African Blackwood
and respect him?

An Ocean of Things

His teeth are stained with salvation.
A woman once told him, 'There is Jesus in your smile'.
His breath smells like a passage I've read late last night.
His tongue heavy with truth
Slicing like a sword to the spines of those who need immediate marrow,
His mouth is surgical in a world where there are more aesthetics than Pell Grants.

Hand me my keys, Purse,
I am headed to the park to meet him.
"I'm here!"
So that we can watch the wind blow through each other's eyelashes,
They rustle like wind chimes into our guardian angel's eardrums
And we call each other love because we know we have it. We do it. We know Him.
"So, hey Love. How you doin'?"

If I could take some days off of work just to vacation in the warmth of your arms,
Your arms would be a linen sling,
Your wrist would be an island,
And your hands would be an ocean of things that I don't deserve for you to give me.

I believe in your love,
And it wouldn't surprise me if there was a world
Beating behind your ribcage
Where people went to their mailboxes in their bathrobes
Because they felt safe enough in the comfort of your affection
To retrieve love letters that I've whispered to your heart while you were sleeping,
Or that I've smashed into your palm while you were speaking.

Understand,
Being faithful is not confined to fidelity, it has a meaning.
It is not exclusive to cheating
Or how long we stay on the phone at night,
It is the boiling point of what we're perfecting, today, measured in Fahrenheit.

If I gathered all of the wrinkles under your eyes
And at the corners of your smile,
They would spell trustworthy on your cheek
So for the record, wherever you are,
My love will be waiting for you when you get there,
Tending to things.
Perhaps maybe even in the next lifetime,

Making sure there are fresh flowers on every table in your mansion

That smell like oils mixed from our fingerprints from
When we held hands in the streets,
In the park,
In the presence of God,

In the future, we will stand before Him
As a preacher pronounces us a name, that will one day,
Be the only thing beautiful about your tombstone,
And we finally smash our smiles together,
Creating kisses that twist like lightning sliding down the back of a tree trunk
And your smile crackles with a sound similar to a waterfall,
A waterfall collapsing under the weight of your dignity and
Spilling into the gulf of your courage.

Communication is an art,
And the ability to effectively communicate is a gift.
But if you forget everything I've said
Just remember, that you have a smile
That I would like for our children to hear over a monitor, one day,
And a laugh designed to cradle the mindset of our mini-mes,
Until the bars of their cribs in their heads
Turn into many trees,

So if you wake up next to a set of eyes that look
like mine, one day,
Just know that that woman
Thinks your wonderful.

You

You...
You give the sun a reason to wake up in the morning,
It's so happy to see you
that it cries tears of fire,
that every nation is forced to physically feel.

You give the wind a reason for dancing,
You are all the proof that I need to believe that
a breeze is what happens when your beauty takes God's breath away,
and the only way some of us survive in the summer
is because He can't keep His eyes off of you.

You are a mountain of a man,
My hands can't help but to dive like eagles over your rocky terrain,
You caress me like a rock slide,
those arms—an avalanche of granite tumbling over my hills,
and if "The hills are alive with...music",
then your fingers are alive with moonshine,
My legs get a little drunk when I'm inside your cocoon ,

Because standing while intoxicated is a thing when

I'm with you,
When we kiss your lips beat on the doors of my
mind like
they're disturbing the peace,
or rather pieces of me that have yet to accept
certain pieces me,
You compliment my world so
my planet isn't content until it makes a resolution,
to drink your lips' electrocution.

I'm under anesthesia when you look my way,
Sleeping beauty, dreaming about the day
I get to breathe in
You.

Songs of You

His neck smells of apples
but his lips are fresh fruit in the orchard of my desires.
Have you seen my love?
He was swimming in my bed sheets
spiced with my lingering perfume,
waist deep in the ocean of my affection,
he glows like the moon.
Have you seen my love?
His thighs are built like emeralds
and his back is a garden of sapphire.
I am looking for my love.

If you see him, look him in his eyes,
respect those two sunflowers springing up,
examining whether there is light in the lamps of your soul.
Shake his hand,
and feel the roughness of his palms—
they shave years of rejection off of the dry walls
I've built around my heart
like sandpaper—
they feel like a pineapple,
and I am his wife
hungry for a taste.

Geometry

Today we fell in love before many,
and these rings on our hands hold a promise that tonight,
We will find out if our inner beauty is actually tangible.
Our love alleviates until our breath abbreviates,
And here we are mining,
Us liquefying,
So like a snagged garment we unravel in each other's arms.

God spread this night sky out like a tent
for us to camp out under His love together.
He is good.
This is good—
though I can't deny your kisses turn my legs into rattlesnake tails every time.
You are an encyclopedia
of everything that is right about being made in the likeness of God.

The geometry of your physique is a sneak peek into how heaven speaks to me.
Those eyes—two trumpets shouting into the recesses of my inner soul.

I am crazy about you,
and maybe that's why your hug is a strait jacket,
because being held by you inadvertently forces me to love myself deeper
And these are the consequences of you perfecting me as a woman.
Thank you for perfecting me as a woman.

Morning Dinner

I caress your face like sunshine
Gnawing at your jawline for breakfast,
Early in the morning we're restless,
So we crawl over each other's limbs until our chests kiss.
Our bodies flip like pages
As we write and make history on these blank sheets,
The clock ticks to the sound of the flames
Popping in our veins' streets.

Let

Let the passion between our kiss burn slow like a cigarette,
Let hands tumble until they find hips,
Let the sun rise
Let the clothes fall
Let the moon bend
Let the stars pour out their brightness
like a bucket full of fire flies,
Let the fire rise
while we're chest to chest,
Let the day break
and spill out rivers of God's best.

Tsunami Skin

Force of nature.
Force of habit.
Tsunami skin.
I gotta grab it.

Human nature.
Human touch.
The things we do.
I'm painted blush.

It's raining for us.
My rainforest.
Gives you the chills.
My body's drowning, in how you make it feel.

Wonder and Grenades

I wonder if candles envy us—
The temperature of this passion between our fingertips— 98.6° times two.
I am 98.6° times you, lips mending to mine like magma
As we float on a matching set of wrinkled vapors that smell like loud linen,
In a place where if pillows talked,
Their lungs would be riddled with your name.
I guess it keeps them soft. I wonder.

I wonder if dogs that get along with cats are filled with the spirit of God.
I wonder if bees sting just to die to get to heaven for a hive that makes honey itself.
Just being in the same room next to you, you won't have to say a word
My hive will make honey itself, your hive will make honey itself,
And you will work and we will sting each other all night until the sun rises,
And you will call me your queen and our skin will reek of pride and high self-esteem.

I am the wind whispering poems into your skin
Until my spirit climbs into your belly button and

holds soliloquies about my inner needs,
Until time gets a taste of this fever
And we're up ten degrees,
And if you think you've seen it all,
All you have to say is please,

Because there are colors locked inside of my chest,
They spill from my lips like lightning,
Only your ears can see them,
My love.
Maybe only your ears can see them. I wonder.

I wonder if star fish freeze because they are imagining what you can do to a spine in a moment of moonlight.
If I am a can of beans and you are a wounded war hero,
I wonder if you're famished.
Are you hungry?
Did you catch that?
Catch it like fingers.
Catch it as if there were taste buds
In the pits of my palms
To satisfy the grip of this hunger I have for you.

We are married therefore midnight rain is not precipitation,
It is simply the moon sweating from how uncomfortable we are making him
By being what we're being,

Making what we're making and having what we have.

You are wonder.
You are thunder.
You are black diamonds in a sauna and your beauty ignites my soul
Like a lightning bolt blistering the belly of a storm cloud.
I envy the way you give me my way
Just to grasp me today,
And I buckle like an IV swallowing a river of liquid roses in your veins.

You have a grenade in your right hand,
I have a grenade in my right hand,
So that we can both get a gist of just how explosive this love really is.
Do you know how explosive this love really is? I wonder.

Not too many things hold the flavor of your name
So sometimes I hum it before I call you to coat my mouth with vibrations that represent you,
Tricking my mind to believe that something as precious as you is inside me
Even for a second.

You're like the first man ever palmed,
Ever calmed by God,
And scattered over the break of day like a psalm by

God.
When you call me, the cadence of your voice moves me like an earthquake,
And I can taste the calligraphy in your tongue every time that your words shape,
So let there be stars, stripes and wonder for your body's my holiday—
A blooming paradise of perfection where all I want to do is stay.

Make Love Like

Ring placed on my left hand,
Desire scorches our souls like soles and desert sand,
So we make love like tornado—
Hips rotating like a ceiling fan in the lap of this mattress,
Make love like a tornado on this mattress.
Make love like coffee—
lips twisting like steam on a cup of your skin,
Make love like a raven—
tongue rap-tap-tapping on my chamber door,
Make love like skin the same color as twelve midnights
melting with the moonlight over every pore.

Make love like magic—
rubbed spines bending over like spoons under thumbs
until voices disappear,
Make love like "Get over here"
And dare lungs to shout whom,
Make love like guns
Like BOOM!
All of that kickback being absorbed in your wrist,
Make love like twist
Like turn,
Like growl,

Like yearn,
Make love like animal
Like roar,
Like hands beating on the chest
Like war.

Make love like after the war your legs will never be the same,
Make love like fire,
Like flame.
Make love like we're too close to care,
Make love like sun
as we splash on this mattress like a solar flare.
Make love like if we don't give it our all tonight we both become extinct,
Make love until our toes are linked,
Make love like pistons,
Like gears
Grinding like gears
Grinding like gears,
Make love like someone tried to kill us but didn't succeed,
Make love until our skin is humming and we're all that we need.

Until the Thunder Rolls

Fire shut up in our bones.
Thunder echoing off of our tongues.
Lightning for limbs.
How do we maintain this tempest we've generated?
I heard sweat is just the way our spirits cry
from all of the energy it takes to become one flesh tonight,
Still I want to love you until the last rain drop drops and the last tear falls
and paint your vertebrae with my bottom lip
until the thunder rolls.

Made in the USA
Columbia, SC
07 February 2022